NATIVE AMERICAN QUOTES

Pueblo- Hold on to what is good, even if it's a handful of earth. Hold on to what you believe, even if it's a tree that stands by itself. Hold on to what you must do, even if it's a long way from here. Hold on to your life, even if it's easier to let it go. Hold on to my hand, even if someday I'll be gone away from you.

Apache- May the sun bring you new energy by day, may the moon softly restore you by night, may the rain wash away your worries, may the breeze blow new strength into your being, may you walk gently through the world and know its beauty all the days of your life.

Blackfoot- What is life? It is the flash of a firefly in the night. It is the breath of a buffalo in the wintertime. It is the little shadow which runs across the grass and loses itself in the sunset.

Chief Aupumut, Mohican- When it comes time to die, be not like those whose hearts are filled with the fear of death, so when their time comes they weep and pray for a little more time to live their lives over again in a different way. Sing your death song, and die like a hero going home.

Wolf Clan Song- There is the world of the flesh, and there is the spirit world. When the flesh is gone, the spirit forever remains. Their voices speak to those who know how to listen. Wisdom is born in the heart, and then spoken.

Cherokee- All life is sacred and all creation related. What we do affects the whole universe. So let us walk in balance with Mother Earth and all her peoples.

Q'ero- Looking behind I am filled with gratitude. Looking forward I am filled with vision. Looking upwards I am filled with strength. Looking within I discover peace.

Cherokee- May the warm winds of Heaven blow softly on your home, and the Great Spirit blesses all who enter there. May your moccasins make happy tracks in many snows, and may the rainbow always touch your shoulder.

Duwamish- There is no death, only a chamber of worlds.

Shikoba- The wild woman has a deep love of nature. A love for the ancient mother, though possibly misunderstood, it has always been in her. When she goes into the wilderness as part of her is soul is going home.

Paiute- A hungry stomach makes a short prayer.

Chief Sitting Bull, Lakota Sioux- Let us put our minds together to see what we can build for our children.

Seneca- He who would do great things should not attempt them alone.

Cherokee- Oh Great Spirit, who made all races, look kindly upon the whole human family and take away the arrogance and hatred which separates us from our brothers.

Cree- Only when the last tree has died and the last river been poisoned and the last fish been caught will we realize we cannot eat money.

Nez Perce- It does not require many words to speak the truth.

Tuscarora- Those who have one foo tin the canoe, and one foot in the boat, are going to fall into the river.

Hopi- Wisdom comes only when you stop looking for it and start living the life the creator intended for you.

Hopi- When the earth is ravaged and the animals are dying, a new tribe of people shall come unto the earth from many colors, creeds and classes, and who by their actions and deeds shall make the earth green again. They shall be known as the warriors of the rainbow.

Mohawk- A good chief gives, he does not take.

Black Elk- Grown men can learn from very little children for the hearts of the little children are pure, therefore, the Great Spirit may show to them many things which older people miss.

Eskimo- You never really know your friends from your enemies until the ice breaks.

Lakota- As you develop your awareness in nature you begin to see how we influence all life and how all life influences us. A key and critical feature for us to know.

Sioux- Speak truth to all people. Only then can you be a true man.

Huron- Listen to the voice of nature, for it holds treasures for you.

Mohawk- Remember that your children are not your own, but are lent to you by the Creator.

Chief Edward Moody, Qwatsinas Nuxalk Nation- We must protect the forests for our children, grandchildren and children yet to be born. We must protect the forests for those who can't speak for themselves such as the birds, animals, fish and trees.

Arapaho- All plants are our brothers and sisters. They to us and if we listen, we can hear them.

Apache- It is better to have less thunder in the mouth and more lightning in the hand.

Tuscarora- Man has responsibility, not power.

Shenandoah- We are made from Mother Earth and we go back to Mother Earth. It is no longer good enough to cry peace, we must act peace, live peace and live in peace.

Cheyenne- Beware of the man who does not talk, and the dog that does not bark.

Navajo- You cannot wake a person who is pretending to be asleep.

Crow- Man's law changes with his understanding of man. Only the laws of the spirit remain always the same.

Blackfoot- What is life? It is the flash of a firefly in the night. It is the breath of a buffalo in the wintertime. It is the little shadow which runs across the grass and loses itself in the sunset.

Lumbee- Seek wisdom, not knowledge. Knowledge is of the past, wisdom is of the future.

Oglala Sioux- To touch the earth is to have harmony with nature.

Dakota- We will be known forever by the tracks we leave.

Eskimo- Those who know how to play can easily leap over the adversaries of life. And one who knows how to sing and laugh never brews.

Shawnee- Each person is his own judge.

Ten Bears, Comanche- I was born upon a prairie where the wind blew free and there was nothing to break the light of the sun. I was born where there were no enclosures and where everything drew a free breath. I want to die there, and not within the walls.

Sauk- You can't purchase friendship- you have to do your part to make it.

Chief Seattle, Suquamish- Humankind has not woven the web of life. We are but one threat within it. Whatever we do to the web, we do to ourselves. All things are bound together. All things connect.

Maori- Turn your face to the sun and the shadows fall behind you.

Cherokee- There is a battle of two wolves inside of us. One is evil. It is anger, jealousy, greed, resentment, lies, inferiority and ego.

The other is good. It is joy, peace, love, hope, humility, kindness, empathy and truth.

Which wolf wins? The one you feed.

Maricopa- Everyone who is successful must have dreamed of something.

Shawnee- We are all one child spinning through Mother Sky.

Onondaga- We give back thanks to our mother, the earth that sustains us.

Ojibway- Sometimes I go about pitying myself, and all the while I am being carried across the sky by beautiful clouds.

Yurok- When you die, you will be spoken of as those in the sky, like the stars.

Cherokee- The weakness of the enemy makes our strength.

Yokuts- My words are tied in one with the great mountains, with the great rocks, with the great trees, in one with my body and my heart. All of you see me, one with this world.

Eskimo- Don't let the windows of your home be so small that the light of the sun cannot enter your rooms.

Tony Ten Fingers, Oglala Lakota- When you are inspired to be and do your best, you find everything is right in your world. Your influence is operating at its highest level and it is the time to influence others in gratitude.

Pueblo- People seeking a myth, will usually find one.

Cherokee- When you were born, you cried and the world rejoiced. Live your life in such a way that when you die the world cries and you rejoice.

Sitting Bull, Lakota- Warriors are not what you think of as warriors. The warrior is not someone who fights because no one has the right to take another's life. The warrior, for us, is one who sacrifices himself for the good of others. His task is to take care of the elderly, the defenseless, those who cannot provide for themselves, above all, the children, and the future of humanity.

Lakota- I see a time of seven Generations when all the colors of mankind will gather under the Sacred Tree of Life and the whole Earth will become one circle again.

Eskimo- Perhaps they are not stars in the sky, but rather openings where our loved ones shine down to let us know they are happy.

Onondaga- There are no secrets or mysteries- there is only common sense.

Arapaho- When we show respect for other living things, they respond with respect for us.

Crow- Old age is not as honorable as death, but most people want it.

Omaha- A man must make his own arrows.

Cheyenne- If a man is as wise as a serpent; he can afford to be as harmless as a dove.

Seneca- Every fire is the same size when it begins.

Iroquois, tribute to Thanksgiving- We return thanks to our mother, the earth, which sustains us. We return thanks to the rivers and streams, which supply us with water. We return thanks to all herbs, which furnish medicines for the cure of diseases. We return thanks to the moon and the stars, which have given to us their light when the sun was gone. We return thanks to the sun, which has looked upon the earth with a beneficent eye. Lastly, we return thanks to the Great Spirit, in who is embodied all goodness and who directs all things for the good of her children.

Seneca- Before leaving your host, give him a little present- it will serve as a little courtesy, and will not offend.

Chief Joseph, Nez Perce- We were taught to believe that the Great Spirit sees and hears everything, and that he never forgets, that hereafter he will give every man a spirit home according to his deserts; If he has been a good man, he will have a good home; if he has a been a bad man, he will have a bad home. This I believe, and all my people believe the same.

Suquamish- All things are connected. Whatever befalls the earth befalls the children of the earth.

Chisca- Treat the earth well: It was not given to you by your parents. It was loaned to you by your children. We do not inherit the Earth from our ancestors; we borrow it from our children.

Blackfoot- Those that lie down with dogs, get up with fleas.

Crow- You already possess everything necessary to become great.

Navajo- Thoughts are like arrows, once released, they strike their mark. Guard them well or one day you may be your own victim.

Cherokee- Listen or your tongue will make you deaf.

Navajo- Coyote is always out there waiting. And coyote is always hungry.

Cheyenne- When you lose the rhythm of the drumbeat; you are lost from the peace and rhythm of life.

Chippewa- I do not think the measure of a civilization is how tall its buildings of concrete are, but rather how well its people have learned to relate to their environment and fellow man.

Cherokee- A woman's highest calling is to lead a man to his soul so as to unite him with source.

A man's highest calling is to protect woman so she is free to walk the earth unharmed.

Choctaw- Certain things catch your eye, but pursue only those that capture the heart.

Omaha- A handsome face does not make a good husband.

Seneca- He who would do great things should not attempt them all alone.

Iowa- A brave man dies but once, a coward many times.

Cheyenne- A good soldier is a poor scout.

Omaha- Dreams are wiser than men.

Chief Luther Standing Bear, Lakota- There is a road in the hearts of all of us, hidden and seldom traveled, which leads to an unknown, secret place. The old people came literally to love the soil, and they sat or reclined on the ground with a feeling of being close to a mothering power. Their teepees were built upon the earth and their altars were made of earth. The soul was soothing, strengthening, cleansing and healing. That is why the old Indian still sits upon the earth instead of propping himself up and away from its life giving forces. For him, to sit or lie upon the ground is to be able to think more deeply and to feel more keenly. He can see more clearly into the mysteries of life and come closer in kinship to other lives about him.

Shoshone- Some people are smart, but not wise.

Omaha- It is easy to show braveness from a distance.

Geronimo, Apache- I cannot think that we are useless or God would not have created us. There is one God looking down on us all. We are all the children of one God. The sun, the darkness, the winds are all listening to what we have to say.

Comanche- All who have died are equal.

Sioux- Religion is for people who are afraid of going to hell. Spirituality is for those who have already been there.

Chief Seattle, Suquamish- You must give to the river the kindness you would give to any brother.

Sioux- Speak truth in humility to all people. Only then can you be a true man.

Chief White Eagle, Ponca- When you are in doubt, be still, and wait; when doubt no longer exists for you, then go forward with courage. So long as mists envelope you, be still; be still until the sunlight pours through and dispels the mists- as it surely will. Then act with courage.

Arapaho- Take only what you need and leave the land as you found it.

Assiniboine- Most of us do not look as handsome to others as we do to ourselves.

Duwamish- Day and night cannot dwell together.

Navajo- A rocky vineyard does not need a prayer, but a pick ax.

Geronimo, Apache- I was no chief and never had been, but because I had been more deeply wronged than others, this honor was conferred upon me, and I resolved to prove worthy of the trust.

Chief Tecumseh, Shawnee- So live your life that the fear of death can never enter your heart. Trouble no one about their religion; respect others in their view, and demand that they respect yours. Love your life, perfect your life, and beautify all things in your life.

Seek to make your life long and its purpose in the service of your people. Prepare a noble death song for the day when you go over the great divide. Always give a word or a sign of salute when meeting or passing a friend, even a stranger, when in a lonely place. Show respect to all people and grovel to none.

When you arise in the morning give thanks for the food and for the joy of living. If you see no reason for giving thanks, the fault lies only in yourself.

Abuse no-one and no thing, for abuse turns the wise ones to fools and robs the spirit of its vision.

Pawnee- What happened in the past and cannot be stopped should not be lamented over.

Eskimo- When a wise man dies, the heavens lament.

Pueblo- I added my breath to your breath that we shall be as one people.

Lakota- Force, no matter how concealed, begets resistance.

Crazy Horse, Oglala- One does not sell the earth upon which people walk.

Hopi- You must live your life from start to finish; no one can do it for you.

Nez Perce- The earth is the mothers of everyone, and everyone should have equal right to it.

Satanta, Kiowa- I love this land and the buffalo and will not part with it. I want you to understand well what I saw. Write it on paper. I hear a great deal of good talk from the gentlemen the Great Father sends us, but they never do what they say. I don't want any of the medicine lodges within the country. I want the children raised as I was. I have heard you intend to settle us on a reservation near the mountains. I don't want to settle. I love to roam over the prairies. There I feel free and happy, but when we settle down we grow pale and die. A long time ago this land belonged to our fathers, but when I go up to the river I see camps of soldiers on its banks. These soldiers cut down my timber, they kill my buffalo and when I see that, my heart feels like bursting.

Lakota- If you continue to contaminate your home, you will eventually suffocate in your own waste.

Omaha- The clear sky and the green fruitful Earth are good; but peace among men is better.

Arapaho- If you wonder often, the gift of understanding will come.

Pueblo- Never sleep while your meat is cooking on the fire.

Blackfoot- There are plenty of different paths to a deep understanding of the universe.

Chief Dan George, Tsleil-Waututh- Love is something you and I must have. We must have it because our spirit feeds upon it. We must have it because without it, we become weak and faint. Without love, our self-esteem weakens. Without it, our courage fails. Without love, we can no longer look out confidently at the world. We turn inward and begin to feed upon our own personalities, and little by little we destroy ourselves.

Cheyenne- Don't judge with the eyes- use the heart instead.

High Eagle, Cherokee- I see the universe; I see myself.

Crow- Stand in the light when you want to assert yourself.

Navajo- A spear is a big responsibility.

Arapaho- May our thoughts reach the sky where there is holiness.

Omaha- Misfortune happens even to the wisest of men.

Suquamish- Every part of the soil is sacred to my people.

Lakota- It is observed that in any great endeavor, it is not enough for a person to depend solely on himself.

Chief Sitting Bull, Sioux- The earth has received the sun's hug, and we shall see the results of that love.

Lumbee- Seek wisdom, not knowledge. Knowledge is of the past, wisdom is of the future.

Shawnee- Respect everyone, but lower yourself to no one.

Cherokee- Listen with your heart. Learn from your experiences, and always be open to new ones.

Chief Yellow Lark, Lakota- O' Great Spirit, whose voice I hear in the winds and whose breath gives life to all the world, hear me! I am small and weak, I need your strength and wisdom. Let me walk in beauty, and make my eyes ever behold the red and purple sunset. Make my hands respect the things you have made and my ears sharp to hear your voice. Make me wise so that I may understand the things you have taught my people. Let me learn the lessons you have hidden in every leaf and rock. I seek strength, not to be greater than my brother, but to fight my greatest enemy, myself. Make me always ready to come to you with clean hands and straight eyes. So when life fades, as the fading sunset my spirit may come to you without shame.

Comanche- A nation is not conquered until the hearts of its women are on the ground. Then it is done, no matter how brave its warriors nor how strong their weapons.

Mohican- Do not pray when it is raining if you do not pray when the sun is shining.

Sioux- The bear, the deer, the great eagle, these are our brothers.

Cherokee- Grandfather, which is more important, to love or to be loved? He replied: Which is more important to the bird, the left wing or the right wing.

Standing Bear, Oglala Sioux Chief- Out of the Indian approach to life there came great freedom, an intense and absorbing respect for life, enriching faith in a supreme power, and principles of truth, honesty, generosity, equality, and brotherhood as a guide to mundane relations.

Nez Perce- Be selective in your battles, sometimes peace is better than being right.

Eskimo- Yesterday is ashes; tomorrow wood. Only today does the fire burn brightly.

Potawatomi- Let us walk softly on the earth with all living beings great and small remembering as we go, that one creator kind and wise created all.

The contributions by Native Americans surrounding knowledge and wisdom runs deep and wide. We are all blessed to be brothers.

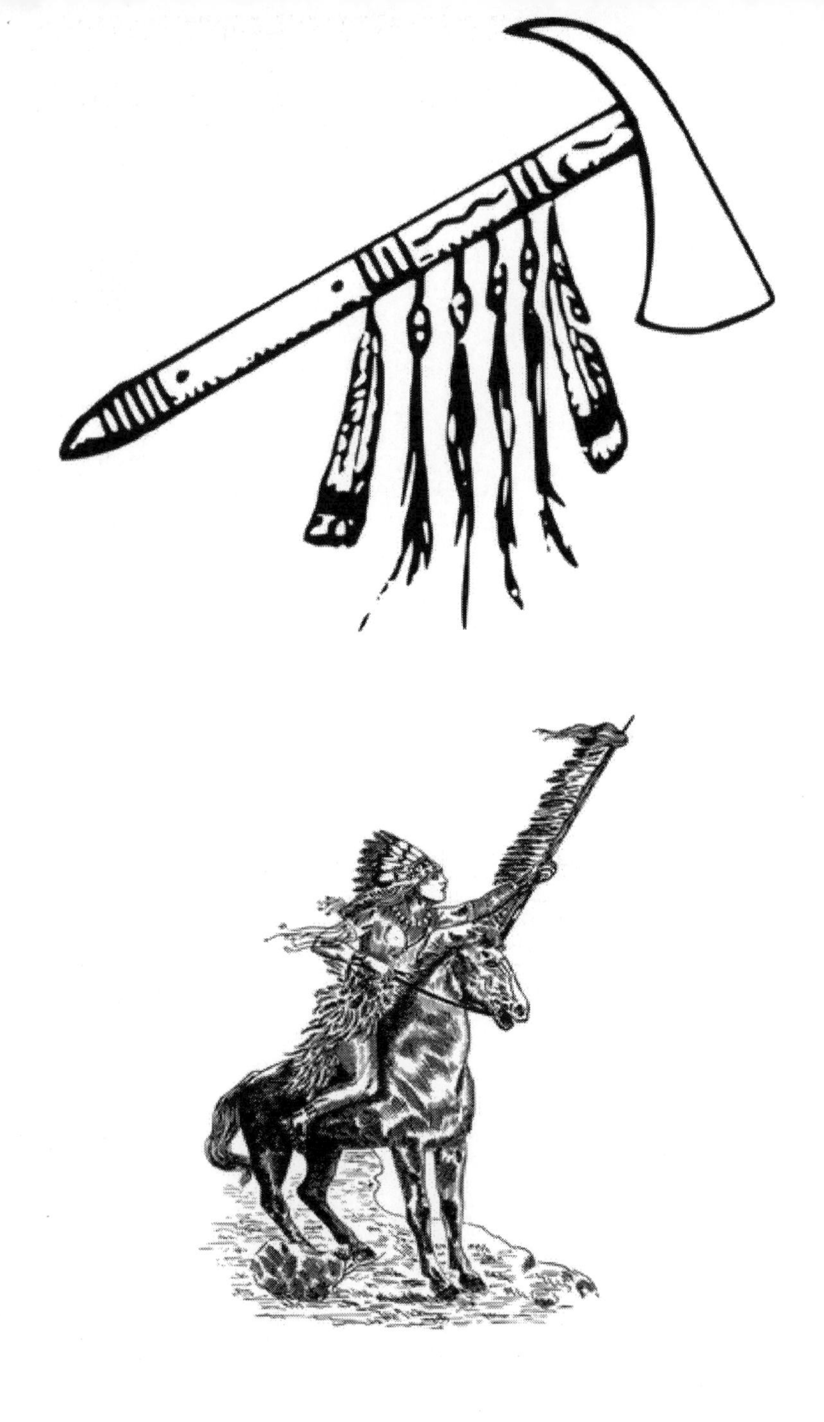

Printed in Great Britain
by Amazon